# Barber shop Bother

Written by Casey Elisha
Illustrated by Lhaiza Morena

Tate and Dad were at the barber shop.

It was time for Tate to get a haircut.

He felt shy.

"Hi! My name is Ash!" the barber said.

"How can I help?"

Tate pointed to a picture.

"Hop in my chair!" Ash said.

Ash lay a white strip on Tate's neck and got him a cape. He tied up some of Tate's hair and got a pair of shiny silver clippers. He started trimming the back and sides.

Suddenly, a bee got near to Tate.

It made him JUMP! Then ...

Ash had cut off a chunk of Tate's hair!

Tate looked in the mirror. He began to cry.

"Sorry!" Ash said. "It was a mistake!"

"What shall we do?" asked Dad.

"We can fix this," said Ash.

"Try his hair in a bun,"
a barber said.

"Try braids!"
said a customer.

"Try spikes!"

"Try a quiff!"

Then Dad said, "I have a plan!"

"What if we cut it all off and give you a fade like mine?" said Dad.

"But what if I do not look good with a fade?" asked Tate.

"You look like me. You will look just fine," Dad said.

Ash got the shiny clippers and started cutting Tate's hair.

Then Ash got an oil sheen spray to make Tate's hair shine.

"Now you and Dad look just like twins!"

Ash said.

Tate and Dad were smiling with pride.